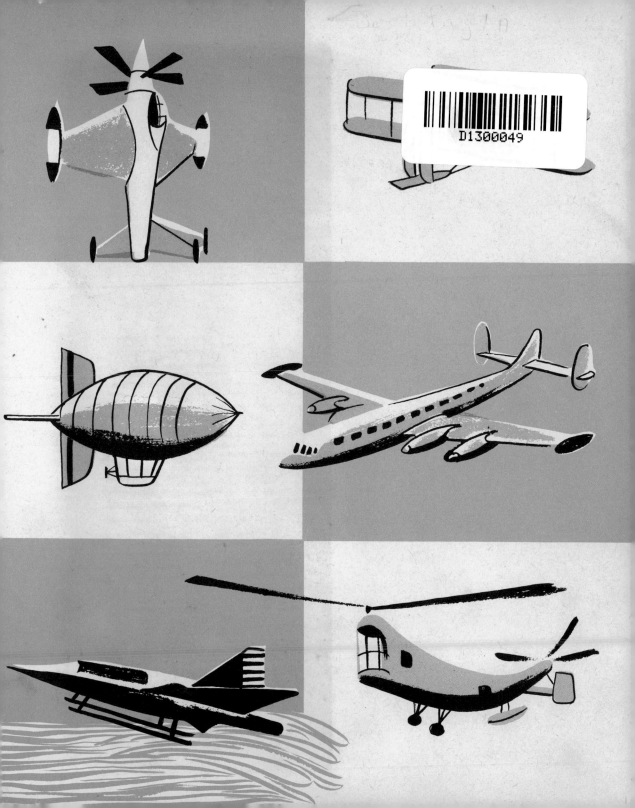

To the Civil Aeronautics Administration,
which makes the air safer for us all.

FIFTH PRINTING

Library of Congress Catalog Card Number: 58-10938

Printed in the United States of America by Polygraphic Company of America

The FIRST BOOK of AIRPLANES

by JEANNE BENDICK

PICTURES BY THE AUTHOR

FRANKLIN WATTS, INC.
575 LEXINGTON AVENUE
NEW YORK 22, N. Y.

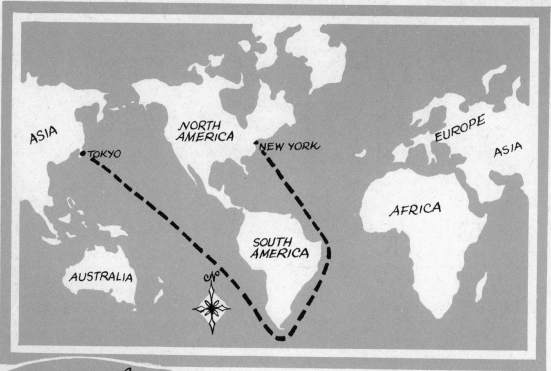

A hundred years ago, you would have traveled the dotted black line from New York to Tokyo.

Air Maps Look Different — The Small World

Here are two maps of the world. You can see that they look very different. One is the kind you usually see in your atlas or geography book. The other is one kind of air map.

Though the shapes of the continents look different on the air map, the maps you are accustomed to seeing do not show them exactly as they are, either. To know what the world really looks like, you must look at a globe. A globe is the best air map there is.

2

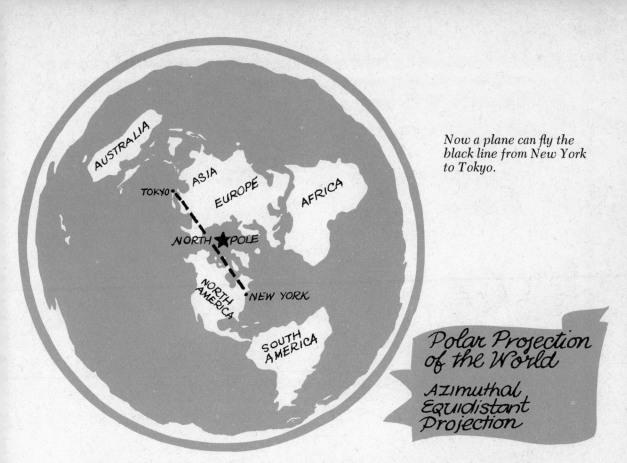

Now a plane can fly the black line from New York to Tokyo.

Polar Projection of the World
Azimuthal Equidistant Projection

For thousands of years, travelers have figured distances between places by the routes they had to use. They had to sail in the sea lanes and travel the roads. Some places were impassable — polar seas, choked with ice that never melts, high mountains, heavy jungles. There were no short cuts through these places.

But planes fly over these obstacles, traveling the shortest distance between two places. If you look at the maps on this page you can see just how much shorter some of the plane routes are. Journeys that used to take weeks (and before that, months and years) can now be made in hours. The big world is becoming very small.

All Kinds of Airplanes

The air above the earth is a roadway for all kinds of planes.
All in one day you might see jets and airliners, helicopters,
cargo planes, small private planes, planes with a wingspread
as long as a football field, and planes with almost no wings at
all.

These airplanes all look different from each other because
they are designed to do different jobs.

Not very long ago there weren't many airplanes. People
rushed out into the street to look up when they heard the

sound of an airplane engine. And not very many years before that, getting an airplane off the ground and into the air for even a few seconds was a marvel.

Now you can see airplanes overhead almost anywhere in the world. In some places they are familiar to people who have never seen a boat or a train or even an automobile.

Ranchers round up cattle in airplanes, farmers dust their crops, mail is delivered, ladies fly to market.

But an airplane, heavier than the air which supports it, is still a wonderful thing. Do you know what makes it fly?

5

What Makes an Airplane Fly?

Two things make an airplane fly.

One of these things is the *engine*, which pushes or pulls the plane through the air.

As the plane flies forward, some air flows under its wings, some air flows over them. *Air* is the other thing that keeps an airplane up.

A car or a train moves over solid ground. Even an ocean liner is lighter than the water that holds it up. Blimps and dirigibles fly because they are filled with a very light gas that makes them lighter than air. But an airplane is tons of heavy metal. How can air hold it up?

You might not be able to see air or feel it, but air is a real thing. The earth is surrounded by an ocean of air.

Just as the water in the sea ocean pushes hard, from all directions, against everything underwater, air pushes hard against all sides of everything it touches, too: people, trees, mountains, houses, airplanes.

Air pushes hard against all sides of everything it touches.

6

The faster air moves, the harder it pushes. Anything that is moving has greater energy (power to do work) than the same thing when it is still.

The plane's engine pulls or pushes it through the air. This pushing or pulling forward is called THRUST.

Because an airplane is solid, it offers resistance to the air moving around it. This resistance is called DRAG. Airplanes are designed to make the air move around them in a certain way. Air has to move faster over the top surface of the wings than over the bottom. In moving faster, the air on the top of the wing presses less than that on the bottom. This difference in pressure lifts the plane up; it is called LIFT.

LIFT and THRUST together make an airplane fly.

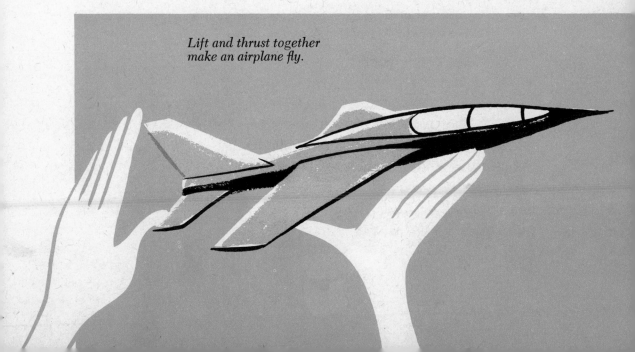

Lift and thrust together make an airplane fly.

About Lift

The wing of an airplane cuts through the stream of air which flows around it just as a boat cuts through the water in which it sails. Some air goes over the wing, some air goes under.

The wing of a plane is shaped this way — curved on top, flat on bottom.

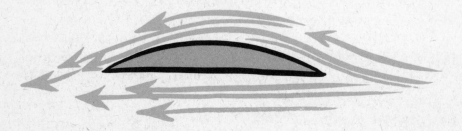

Since the stream of air that flows over the curved top of the wing has to travel a longer distance than the air flowing past the straight under surface, it has to move faster to catch up. The pressure on the top of the wing drops, and this creates lift on the top of the wing. About three-quarters of all the lift on the plane is created this way. Lift holds the plane up.

About Thrust

When you are swimming, your arms and hands push the water back, and you go forward. If you have a good strong kick you can go forward without even moving your arms and hands. Your kick pushes you forward through the water.

You push the water back,

and you go forward.

If the plane has propellers, the propeller blades bite into the air, pulling the plane forward in much the same way your arms and hands pull you forward when you swim. As the propellers pull the air into them and back over the wings, they pull the plane forward.

The propeller pulls the air back,

and the plane goes forward.

A jet engine pushes the plane forward more in the way you go through the water on your strong kick alone. A jet engine shoots out behind it a strong stream of air that pushes the plane forward.

The forward motion of the plane pushing through the air is its THRUST.

The stream of air from the jet pushes it forward.

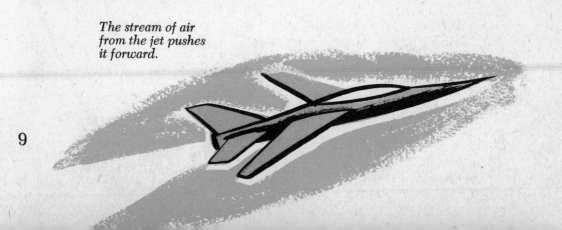

The Parts of a Plane

An airplane doesn't have the kind of steering wheel a car or a boat has. The pilot steers a plane with a long handle that sticks up out of the floor. This handle is called the STICK. In some planes the stick may have only a knob on top. In other planes it has a sort of half-wheel.

The stick is connected to the movable parts of the plane's tail, which are called ELEVATORS. The elevators go up and down.

Pulling the stick *back* makes the elevators go *up*. This makes the tail of the plane go *down*, and the nose goes up in the air. The plane climbs.

Pushing the stick *forward* makes the elevators go *down*. Then the tail goes *up* and the nose of the plane points toward the ground. The plane heads down.

The stick is also connected to the movable parts of the wings, which are called AILERONS. Pushing the stick to the left or right

10

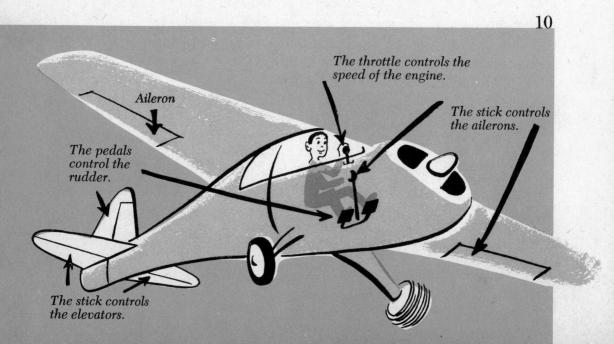

The throttle controls the speed of the engine.

Aileron

The stick controls the ailerons.

The pedals control the rudder.

The stick controls the elevators.

(or turning the half-wheel on the end of the stick) makes one aileron go down and the other go up. This makes the plane slant in one direction or the other. Fliers call this BANKING the plane. Banking makes turning easier.

The pilot uses his feet, too. On the floor are two PEDALS, fastened to a bar called the RUDDER BAR. The rudder bar is connected to the rudder in the plane's tail. Stepping on the *left pedal* makes the plane turn to the *left*. Stepping on the *right pedal* makes it turn to the *right*.

All the movable parts of the plane's wings and tail are called the CONTROL SURFACES.

A handle called the THROTTLE is connected to the plane's engine. The more the throttle is open, the more fuel goes into the engine and the faster the engine turns. The throttle, the stick, and the pedals are the controls with which the pilot guides his plane.

The picture shows you where these and all the other parts of a plane are.

11

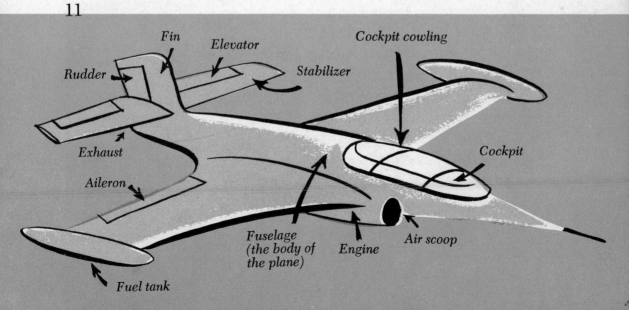

Fin
Elevator
Cockpit cowling
Rudder
Stabilizer
Exhaust
Cockpit
Aileron
Fuselage (the body of the plane)
Engine
Air scoop
Fuel tank

How Airplane Engines Work

Most airplanes, except for military planes and some airliners, are driven by PROPELLERS. Their engines are called RECIPROCATING ENGINES, and they work like this.

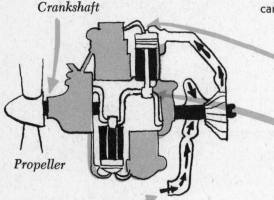

RECIPROCATING ENGINE

Crankshaft

Propeller

Air intake

Air comes into the engine from outside and is mixed with gasoline vapor in the carburetor.

A spark plug in the cylinder ignites the mixture of air and gas, which expands as it burns, pushing hard against the piston and forcing it down in the cylinder.

The cylinder is joined to a connecting rod, which turns the crankshaft, which turns the propeller.

Of course one cylinder couldn't turn the propeller by itself. Some planes have as many as 24 cylinders; smaller planes have fewer. Many airplane engines have the cylinders arranged in a circle instead of in a straight row, as they are in an automobile engine. Engines with this circular arrangement of pistons are called RADIAL ENGINES.

RADIAL ENGINE

Reaction Engines

A jet engine is called a REACTION ENGINE. A pure reaction engine has no propeller. A reaction engine pushes a plane through the air because rapidly expanding gases push hard against the closed front of the cylinder. Unable to escape there, they bounce back and shoot out of the exhaust at the rear, pushing the plane forward.

The simplest kind of jet engine is the RAMJET. It works like this.

Air comes into the front and is compressed.

RAMJET ENGINE

Fuel is vaporized into the compressed air and ignited. This ignition heats the air and makes it expand.

The heated air rushes out of the exhaust at a terrific speed.

Because it has no mechanical parts, the speed of a ramjet is almost unlimited. (There is a limit to how fast mechanical parts can move.) But most ramjets have to be going fast to start working, because air must be rushing through the engine to burn the fuel, and to push the hot air out the back. And because the air shutter at the front opens and closes, the thrust is not as smooth as it is in other reaction engines.

13

Many jet planes have TURBOJET engines. Like a ramjet, a turbojet has no propeller. A turbojet engine works like this.

TURBOJET ENGINE

Air comes in through the air inlet.

It flows into the compressor, where its pressure is increased.

Then it is forced into the combustion chamber, where it is mixed with fuel vapor, and burned.

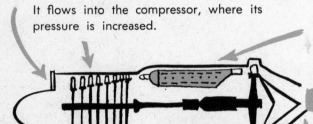

The burning gas expands through the turbine and is forced out the tail cone at a terrific speed.

A TURBOPROP engine looks like a turbojet, except that the turbine is larger and heavier because it has an extra job to do. It spins a propeller. Both the propeller and the exhaust provide the thrust for a plane with a turboprop engine.

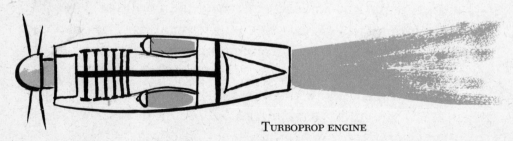

TURBOPROP ENGINE

14

A ROCKET engine is a reaction engine too, but it does not need to scoop in air from outside as the jet engines do. It carries not only its fuel, but the oxygen to burn it.

A rocket engine works like this.

The fuel and oxygen are injected into a burning chamber.

When very hot gases push hard against the wall of the chamber, they are thrown back out of the exhaust, so pushing the plane ahead.

Fuel   *Oxygen*

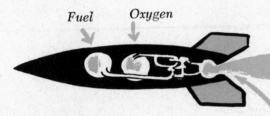

ROCKET ENGINE

Burning chamber

Because rocket engines do not need air from outside, they will probably power the aircraft that travel in space, where there is no air.

Scientists are working on other kinds of engines too — on a nuclear engine that will have an atomic reactor for releasing the power of uranium to make the plane run.

Scientists are even working on a solar engine so that rockets can make use of the great chemical stores of solar energy (energy from the sun) that are available in space.

Leonardo's flying machine

The first non-rigid airship

Some Airplane History

Since the earliest times, men have dreamed of flying. Back in the sixteenth century, Leonardo da Vinci made a plan for a flying machine. (He invented the parachute, too.) But it was almost three hundred years before anyone figured out a way really to get up into the air.

The first flying machines were balloons, filled with hot air or hydrogen, which is a very light gas. The balloons went up because both hot air and hydrogen are lighter than air. Our present-day blimps and dirigibles fly because they are filled with another very light gas, helium.

The first airship that could actually be steered in any direction, no matter which way the wind blew, was a sort of blimp, driven by an electric motor. Its name was *La France,* and it flew in 1884.

For many years inventors had been experimenting with gliders, which were the first flying ships with wings, and many glider flights were made. Otto Lilienthal's gliders were very

The Wright brothers' first successful plane

One of Lilienthal's gliders

An early helicopter

Glenn Curtiss' first seaplane

successful. The wing tops were curved, like those of modern airplanes.

In 1903 the Wright brothers built the first motor-driven airplane that really flew. It was in the air for 12 seconds, and it flew 120 feet. Orville Wright lay on the lower wing and steered with his hands and feet.

In 1906 Alberto Santos-Dumont built the first plane to take off under its own power.

The year 1907 brought the first successful helicopter flight. The helicopter rose one foot into the air on its first trial.

The year 1911 was a busy one in airplane history. The first radio message was sent from a plane. There was the first demonstration of bombing from a plane. An airplane landed on the deck of a ship for the first time, and the first seaplane flight was made.

During World War I much was learned about flying and planes. After the war, the first air mail service was started. Airplanes flew around the world and over the ocean.

The first trip around the world in 1924 took six months. Now the same trip can be made in hours.

17

Wilbur and Orville Wright

These Men and Planes Made Air History

Orville and Wilbur Wright made the first successful power-driven flight in 1903.

Leon Delagrange was the first pilot to take up a passenger, in 1908.

Glenn Curtiss

After the Wrights, Glenn Curtiss was the greatest of the American flying pioneers. He designed many of the best early engines, built the first practical seaplane, and was the first to think of the airplane carrier.

In 1909 Mme. la Baronne de Laroche became the first woman pilot.

Blériot flies the English Channel.

In 1909, Louis Blériot was the first to fly the English Channel. He was hardly ever more than a few feet above the water.

In 1912 Sir Alliott-Verdon Roe, a British designer, built the first plane with an enclosed cabin.

18

This was the first Army airplane, 1911.

This was the first scheduled airliner, in 1914.

General "Billy" Mitchell first realized the strategic importance of air power.

In 1927 Charles Lindbergh made the first solo non-stop flight over the Atlantic Ocean.

In 1933 Wiley Post made the first solo flight around the world, in less than 8 days.

Igor Sikorsky was a helicopter pioneer. He perfected the helicopter 30 years after his first trials.

Major Charles Yeager was the first man to fly faster than sound.

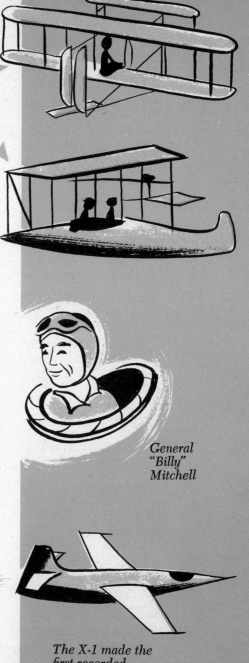

General "Billy" Mitchell

The X-1 made the first recorded flight faster than sound.

19

Airports

An AIRPORT is to a plane what a safe harbor is to a ship. It is a place where a pilot can take off on a journey, and return safely when the journey is over.

Some airports may have only a single HANGAR with a WIND-SOCK on top (to blow with the wind and show the pilot the wind direction), and one RUNWAY in front.

In some places an airport may be only a barn with a wind-sock, and a road for a runway.

But a big airport is a very special kind of place. It has many hangars, and places for repairing and checking planes. It has an AIR TERMINAL through which travelers pass on their way to many different places all over the world. It has shops and restaurants and maybe even a movie theater and a hotel where travelers can stay if there is a delay between planes.

The runways of a big airport stretch out in many directions, sometimes for miles. They are built in this way so that planes can always take off and land into the wind. With the wind blowing toward them, across their wings, planes get extra lift to help them take off. And when a plane comes in, the head wind, pushing against it, keeps it from landing too fast. The wind provides extra lift to keep the plane up while it is flying slowly, too.

20

At the airport there is a RADAR TOWER that sends out electronic waves in all directions. When the waves touch a plane in the air, they bounce back to a screen in the airport, and make a kind of picture of whatever they touch. The radar men can look at the screen and tell just where planes are in the air, and how fast they are coming.

A great many people work at a large airport. Mechanics are there to check and fix the engines of the planes. Metalworkers mend any other parts that might be broken. A weatherman, called a meteorologist, keeps a constant check on the weather. He watches the WIND INDICATOR to see which way the wind is blowing. He watches the ANEMOMETER to see how fast the wind is blowing. He watches the BAROMETER to see what the air pressure is, because a change in air pressure means a change in the weather.

There are people at the airport to figure out schedules, to load freight and baggage, to sell tickets, to paint hangars, fix runways, and direct the pilots when they are moving their planes around on the ground. There are usually a post office and an express office.

But the heart of an airport, the most important place, is the CONTROL TOWER.

21

The Control Tower

The control tower is usually on top of the biggest building at the airport. Sometimes it has a tower all to itself. All the walls of the control tower room are made of glass, so that the people who work there can look in every direction. The glass is specially made so that the sun can never get in anybody's eyes.

On top of the control tower are the weather instruments and the AIRPORT BEACON, which is a sort of lighthouse for planes. Airport beacons all flash green light, then white, so pilots can identify them without any trouble.

The Civil Aeronautics Administration, which is a part of the United States Department of Commerce, has charge of the control towers at most of the United States airports. The CAA (as it is called for short) trains and licenses all control tower operators, and is, in a way, their boss.

The control tower operator is the captain of the airport. All the pilots, military or civilian, who fly in and out of that airport must obey his orders. Even pilots from foreign countries must be able to understand what he says. A big airport has a number of controllers. Each one does a different job. The planes landing and taking off every few seconds would bump into each other if their pilots did not obey the controllers' orders exactly.

Sometimes the controller has to keep a number of planes circling above the field at different altitudes, each plane waiting for a turn to land. He calls this "stacking them up."

Every airport has its own FLIGHT PATTERN, a certain way planes must approach it. When they are ten miles from the airport, the planes come into its CONTROL AREA. At three miles, they are in the airport's TRAFFIC ZONE. Even if there are dozens of planes stacked up, none of them bump because they all fly in their own places in the pattern, in just the way the control tower operator tells them to.

The men in the control tower have many ways to help the pilots in their planes, even when they cannot see the planes at all. The controllers and the pilots are connected not only by their radios, over which they can talk back and forth, but by electronic instruments in the control tower and on the instrument panel in front of the pilot.

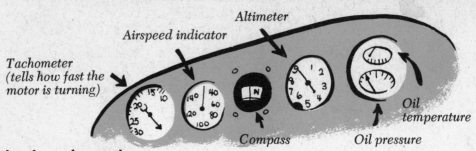

Tachometer
(tells how fast the
motor is turning)

Airspeed indicator

Altimeter

Oil
temperature

Compass

Oil pressure

Help for the Pilots

The instrument panel of a small plane looks very much like the dashboard of a car. Each of the dials shows something the pilot needs to know — how fast the plane is flying through the air, how fast the engine is turning, how far above sea level the plane is flying. The pilot has to know his direction, how hot the engine is, the oil pressure, how much gas is in the tank.

But the pilots who fly large planes or jets need more help than this. They fly long distances, in all kinds of weather. Some fly so fast that once they see something in their way, even if it is many miles off, there is no time to avoid it.

One of a pilot's best assistants is his radar screen. Radar can see through night and fog. It can see approaching planes or mountains in the dark long before the pilot sees them. It can even see stormy weather ahead.

A dial which works on a radio beam shows the pilot when he is flying on course, and tells him the instant he goes off.

When he is on course, the dial looks like this.

If he goes off, it looks like this.

The same dial has a horizontal needle too. When the pilot wants to come in for a landing, he tunes in on

24

the airport's INSTRUMENT LANDING SYSTEM. By keeping the two pointers crossed, exactly in the center, the pilot can land smoothly on the runway. The controller watches the plane's approach on radar, too, and can talk to the pilot on the radio.

There is even a "no hands" automatic landing device that will land the plane safely without any help from the pilot at all. There is an automatic pilot, too, which keeps the plane flying on course even if no one is at the controls.

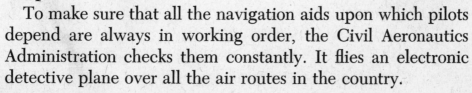

The pilot's radio keeps him in constant touch with the airports, control points, and weather stations on the ground below. Large planes have several radios. Some connect the plane to the ground and some connect the crew members in different parts of the plane.

To make sure that all the navigation aids upon which pilots depend are always in working order, the Civil Aeronautics Administration checks them constantly. It flies an electronic detective plane over all the air routes in the country.

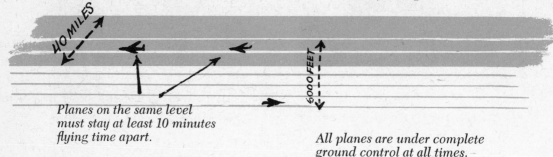

Along the most heavily traveled sky roads all planes fly along an imaginary skyway that is 40 miles wide.

They fly at levels 1,000 feet apart, starting 17,000 feet high.

Planes on the same level must stay at least 10 minutes flying time apart.

All planes are under complete ground control at all times.

Roads in the Sky

The sky looks very big, and it is. It looks as if there were room in it for all the planes that ever flew, with room to spare. It is hard to imagine a traffic jam in the sky, but jams happen over big cities and many airports. And since most planes travel along the same "roads" in the sky, they must obey very strict traffic rules.

Planes flying south and west fly at *even* altitudes — maybe 4,000 or 6,000 feet. Planes flying north and east fly at *odd* altitudes — maybe 5,000 or 7,000 feet. The main routes have color names, and every pilot knows which color route he is flying. Planes flying on the *green* airway always have the right of way. *Amber* is next, then *red*, then *blue*. Wherever air highways cross, all pilots know who has right of way.

Safety Rules

The Civil Aeronautics Administration assists private planes, airlines planes, and military planes, and it has made very strict safety rules which their pilots must obey exactly. If a pilot disobeys *any* of these rules, a report slip goes in to the CAA about it, so that the CAA can decide what to do about that pilot.

Maybe you have thought to yourself that it would be fun to have your own plane so that you could jump into it any time you wanted to, and fly off in any direction that looked pretty. Well, sometimes you can. But under certain conditions, before you can fly anywhere you have to tell the CAA where you are going, what route you are going to fly, when you plan to take off, and when you plan to land. This information is called your FLIGHT PLAN. When you land, you must call and report your landing promptly. Pilots of airliners and military planes have to report at certain places along their routes, while they are flying.

There are other safety rules, too. Pilots must fly at least 500 feet above the ground in the country, much higher over towns, and still higher over cities.

At night all planes must show a *white* light on their tails, a *red* light on the tip of their left wing and a *green* light on the tip of their right wing. These lights show other pilots which way the plane is going. The lights blink, too, so nobody can mistake them for stars.

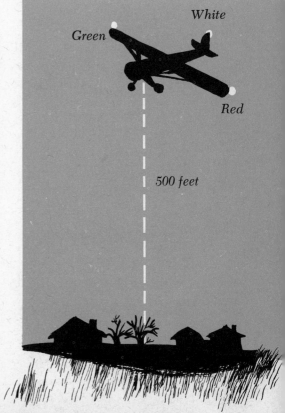

27

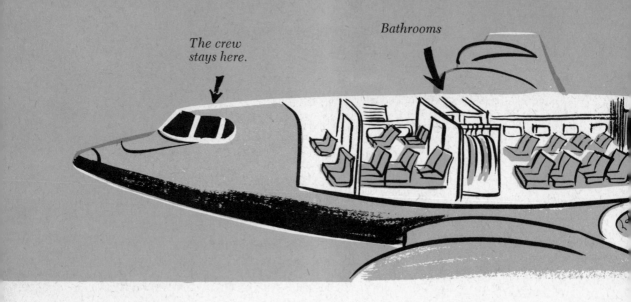

The crew stays here.

Bathrooms

Airliners

Some airliners are like hotels in the sky. They have an upstairs and a downstairs. They have berths for sleeping, and a kitchen (called a galley) for fixing food. They have bathrooms and dressing rooms, closets and a clubroom. You can walk around or sleep or have dinner while you are flying along at hundreds of miles an hour.

Every airliner has a crew that has been especially trained. There are a PILOT and a COPILOT. They sit next to each other in the cockpit and take turns flying the plane. Each pilot has a complete set of controls. When one is flying, the other can walk around a little or eat. When the pilot is taking off or landing, the copilot has other jobs, such as putting the landing gear up and down.

28

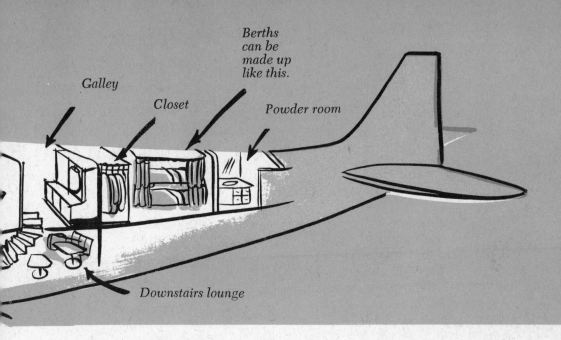

Galley

Closet

Berths can be made up like this.

Powder room

Downstairs lounge

Most four-engine airliners have a FLIGHT ENGINEER who checks all the engines and other equipment. Airliners that fly over the ocean have a NAVIGATOR and a RADIO MAN, too. And all airliners have at least one STEWARD or STEWARDESS, and sometimes two or three, to fix and serve dinner and make the passengers comfortable.

Before an airliner leaves the ground — even before the passengers come aboard — many people work to get the plane ready. It is carefully checked to make sure everything is working perfectly. The inside is scrubbed and cleaned and vacuumed. Blankets are neatly folded on the racks, clean cases are put on the pillows, the drinking tanks are filled. There is a lot of housekeeping on an airliner.

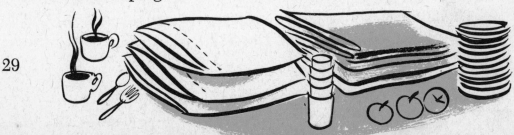

A little while before the plane takes off, the baggage truck rolls up. Then the baggage men load the baggage and mail into the CARGO SPACE, through a door in the bottom of the plane. Pets have to ride in the cargo space, too.

A gasoline truck puts gas into the big tanks in the wings of the plane — enough gas to get the plane where it is going, with plenty to spare.

Another truck unloads food right into the galley. Because the galley is too small for cooking so many dinners, everything is cooked ahead of time and loaded into big steel cabinets that keep it hot until serving time — even overnight.

When it is time for the passengers to come aboard, each one shows his ticket at the gate. Each passenger's name is checked so that everybody gets on the right plane. Otherwise someone who thought he was going to Chicago might find himself in Boston before he finished reading his paper.

When everybody is in, the door is closed and locked from the outside. The big staircase that was rolled up to the plane is moved away.

The pilot and copilot start the engines one at a time. They listen to instructions from the control tower, telling them which runway to use for taxiing (when a plane rolls along the ground it is taxiing) and which runway to use for taking off.

When the plane is in the air, nobody except the crew is allowed in the cockpit. The crew have all kinds of instruments to help them, to show them what the weather is up ahead and where the smoothest flying is, and to guide the plane safely into the airport even if they can't see a foot ahead of them. They can talk over the radio to the control towers and weather stations along the way.

If you are an airline passenger you have many things to make you comfortable besides the soft chairs and good things to eat. The cabin is pressurized so that you won't feel changes in the air pressure when the plane goes miles up, then comes down. The cabin is heated, too, so that you are warm even if the temperature outside the plane is below zero.

Sometimes, looking down, you can see cities and houses that look like toys, roads and rivers that look like ribbons, lakes that look like silver trays in the sun. Sometimes you can see only clouds below, like cotton candy or fairy cities. Sometimes you can see green fields and deserts and snow all in the same day. And at night you can see the stars brighter than you ever have before.

31

Flying Freight

Airplanes carry a great deal of freight. Some freight can travel more slowly, by truck or train or boat, and some freight is too big or heavy for a plane. But some things have to get where they are going in a hurry.

Some cargo planes look like airliners. Some are so big they look like dirigibles with wings. They have six pusher engines, and ten huge wheels to land on. They have big elevators in the bottom, which let down to hoist cargo into the hold. And they have ramps, so that wheeled equipment can roll right in. One cargo plane has a front that opens like a huge mouth to swallow the freight. The whole cargo section of another slides out, so the plane itself doesn't have to wait for unloading — the cargo section can be unhitched, like a box car.

32

Shipments of medicine and vaccines travel by air, and so does perishable food, like fresh fish, and fancy fruit. Flowers are flown from Hawaii to the United States. Horses and prize cattle are flown across continents and even across oceans. Baby chicks are shipped by air, and so are all kinds of queer animals for zoos.

Heavy machinery is flown into remote places. In some mountainous parts of South America all the machinery needed for mining is flown in. Once it had to be shipped by sea. Then weeks were spent, getting it from the seaport to the mines. It had to be taken apart, loaded on mules, carried up and down mountains, and finally put back together again. Now, in just a day or two, the same machinery gets from the factory where it is made, to the place where it will go to work.

Even whole soda fountains are shipped by air. They arrive all assembled, and ready to go to work as soon as the ice cream can be loaded in.

Cargo planes carry automobiles and statues, food, clothing and newspapers, costumes and scenery for plays. Nowadays even elephants fly.

Planes Do All Kinds of Work

Many kinds of small planes are used for many different jobs. Most small planes have one engine, driven by a propeller. Some seat only two people, some as many as five.

Planes For Cars

In some parts of the country, where people live far apart, they sometimes use airplanes the way they would a family car. Ladies fly in to town to market, farmers fly in to buy their supplies, doctors make their calls by plane.

Even where people live closer together, business men fly from one factory to another or from town to town and back the same day.

Whoever pilots a private plane must have a flying license, just as an automobile driver must have a driving license. He has to obey the same rules and know the same safety regulations that the pilot of an airliner or a jet fighter does.

The Flying Farmers

Many modern farmers use planes to help them. On very large farms they even plant seeds from the air — miles of rice or wheat in one day. The same planes can be used to spray crops. There is a big tank in the plane, and by pressing a lever the pilot can spray acres of apple trees or corn or other grain so that the bugs won't eat them. He can spray oil over swamps to kill mosquitoes, too.

In the winter, when scattered cattle are cut off from food by a big snowstorm, ranchers sometimes fly the range and drop bales of hay wherever they see groups of cattle. And at roundup time they use planes to herd the cattle together for branding and separating.

Flying the Bush

In Alaska and parts of Canada and in countries like Australia, towns and houses are far apart and there are often no trains and buses between places. Here, bush pilots and their planes are the railroad, the telephone, the grocery truck and even the newspaper.

35

Bush pilots do their flying in wild country, instead of from airport to airport. They bring supplies to villages and to logging and mining camps. They carry news and messages from one village to another. Sometimes they fly medicine or doctors or pieces of machinery. If there is heavy snow, the planes have skiis instead of wheels.

Flying Forest Rangers

Forest rangers use small planes, and sometimes helicopters, to help them all year round. In summer and autumn, when the forests are very dry, the flying rangers spend most of their time looking for forest fires. They fly over miles of forest, on the lookout for a glow or a wisp of smoke.

If a pilot finds a fire he calls back on his radio to tell the nearest ranger station where it is, and what equipment to bring. Sometimes it is difficult to get fire fighters close to the fire in a hurry with their trucks and tanks.

Then a bigger plane or a helicopter flies over, and specially trained fire fighters, called smoke jumpers, parachute down close to the fire so that they can get started before the rest of the equipment arrives. These flying fire engines drop chemicals on the fire too, to help put it out.

In the spring, when there is hardly any chance of fire, flying rangers sometimes carry tanks of baby fish in a seaplane. They fly low over lakes and streams and dump thousands of fish out through the bottom of the plane into the water.

Flying rangers also use their planes to hunt for people who are lost in wild territory.

Flying Prospectors

Maybe when you think of a prospector you think of an old sourdough in a battered hat, with a pickax over one shoulder, and all his equipment loaded on his faithful mule. Some prospectors may still look like this, but many modern prospectors, especially those searching for uranium, do their prospecting in airplanes.

Uranium always gives off radiations. If a prospector has a detector, a Geiger counter or an oscillator, he doesn't have to see uranium to know when it is there. He can fly low in his plane, over territory that is so wild it would take days or weeks to cover on foot, and in a few hours he can mark off all the places on his map where the detector has registered. Then he can return by jeep and explore those places more carefully, without wasting time on the places that showed no radiation.

The Rain Makers

Sometimes, when rain has been badly needed for a long time, a pilot will turn his plane into a rain-making machine. When the meteorologist says the clouds are right, the pilot goes up and "seeds" them with a special chemical. And sometimes this seeding does make the clouds drop their rain.

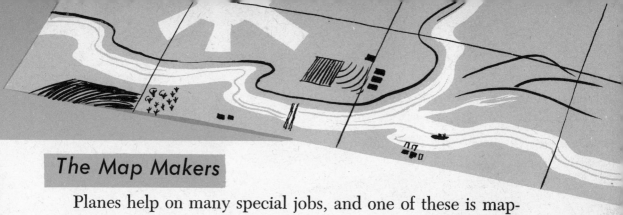

The Map Makers

Planes help on many special jobs, and one of these is map-making. Cameras in the bottom of the plane continuously photograph the country over which they are flying. When the pictures they take are pasted together, they make a super-giant photograph of the country, big enough so that the map makers can see every detail.

The Hurricane Hunters

Hurricanes and typhoons are tremendous storms that can cause immense damage and loss of life. Once there was no way of telling when these storms were coming until the barometer started to drop, just before the storm hit. Now airplanes hunt them down.

When the hurricane hunters see a suspicious storm forming, they keep constant watch on it. They fly right through the storm center with special equipment to measure its pressures, the speed of its winds, and its direction. Then they can warn the people in its path to get ready, before the storm arrives.

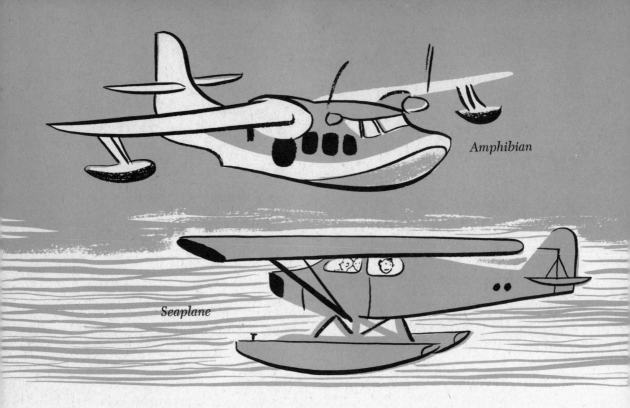

Amphibian

Seaplane

Seaplanes, Amphibians, and Flying Boats

Some planes are built so that they can take off or come down on either land or water. They are called AMPHIBIANS (just as the animals are who can live either on land or in the water).

An amphibian plane's hull is shaped like a roundish boat bottom, and usually the plane lands on its hull. Under the wing tips are small floats called STABILIZERS, which keep the wings from going underwater if the plane tilts a little in landing or taking off. If the amphibian's pilot wants to come down on land, he can make wheels pop out of the bottom of the hull. One kind of Navy amphibian has a boat hull, wheels, floats, and skis, so that it can land anywhere in the world. Planes like this Navy amphibian supply bases in the Arctic and Antarctic.

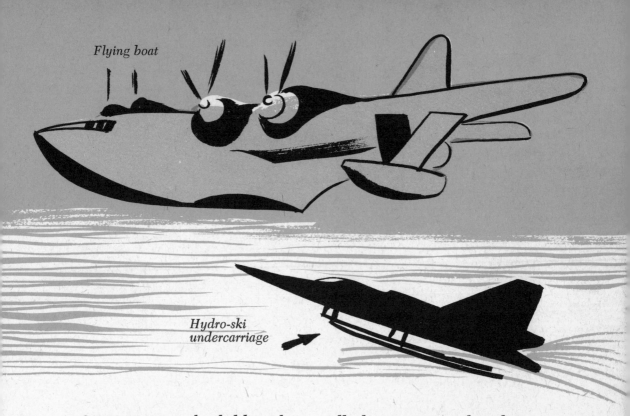

Flying boat

Hydro-ski undercarriage

SEAPLANES are built like other small planes, except that they have floats instead of wheels. Seaplane pilots have to land on lakes, oceans, or rivers instead of runways. Seaplanes are often used by sportsmen to fly to out-of-the-way places where the fishing is good. Sometimes canoes are strapped right onto the floats.

Some of the biggest planes in the world are FLYING BOATS. Their wings are so big they have tunnels inside them where mechanics can work. Some of them even carry a small seaplane on top, just as a ship carries a rowboat.

Some very fast Navy seaplanes have a hydro-ski undercarriage, like the one above. They can take off and land very fast, even when the water is quite rough.

Helicopters

HELICOPTERS can do many things that winged airplanes cannot do. Helicopters have no wings. They get their lift from three or four long ROTOR BLADES, mounted on top. The rotors whirl around like an electric fan and make the helicopter fly. By changing the slant or pitch of the rotor blades, the pilot can make the helicopter go forward or back or straight up. He can even make it stand still in the air. On the tail of the helicopter there is a propeller to steady it.

Helicopters don't need runways for taking off or landing. They can go straight up from a very small place, and they can land almost anywhere — on top of a mountain, on a roof, or the deck of a ship. Because they can land like this they are handy for many kinds of jobs where other aircraft would be useless. But helicopters cannot fly as fast as winged airplanes can, or go as high.

The Coast Guard and Harbor Police use helicopters for making rounds in crowded harbors and along shorelines where there are many pleasure boats. Because helicopters can fly so slowly, and even stand still for a better look, they are good trouble-spotters. If the pilot sees a boat in trouble he calls the Harbor Police or the Coast Guard on his radio, and they send a fast boat to the rescue. But if the people need to be rescued right away, the pilot can come down next to them and pick them up.

Sometimes State Police use helicopters, too. They are very handy for straightening out traffic jams. The helicopter policeman can fly over the snarl and see just what is holding things up. Then he can direct traffic until everything is straightened out. Sometimes police use helicopters for chasing lawbreakers who are trying to make a getaway.

Some fire companies have helicopter assistants. They use them in place of big extension ladders, or where the ladders won't reach. The firemen on the pumping truck hand the hose

up to a fireman in the helicopter. Then he flies the hose up to the top of the building and shoots water down into the fire.

During World War II, helicopters were used for the first time as emergency ambulances. They could fly into remote spots and take wounded soldiers out quickly and easily, back to the nearest hospital. They are used in this same way in peacetime disasters. Helicopter ambulances can carry three stretchers strapped to the outside of the plane, and sometimes one inside.

Helicopters carry air mail from post offices to the airport. They take off from the post office roof and land right at the airport post office. They also carry mail to ships at sea.

Helicopters make good taxis. Many airports have helicopter service to and from the airport, so that airline passengers can travel above the crowded roads. Sometimes the drive by car from an airport into town takes longer than the flight from one city to another has.

There are helicopter taxi services, too, that take business people from the suburbs where they live into the cities where they work.

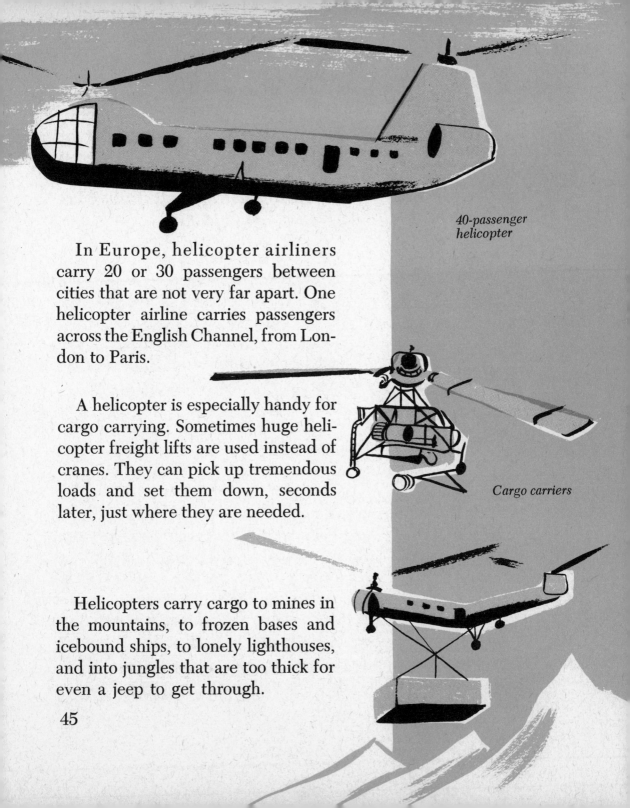

*40-passenger
helicopter*

In Europe, helicopter airliners carry 20 or 30 passengers between cities that are not very far apart. One helicopter airline carries passengers across the English Channel, from London to Paris.

A helicopter is especially handy for cargo carrying. Sometimes huge helicopter freight lifts are used instead of cranes. They can pick up tremendous loads and set them down, seconds later, just where they are needed.

Cargo carriers

Helicopters carry cargo to mines in the mountains, to frozen bases and icebound ships, to lonely lighthouses, and into jungles that are too thick for even a jeep to get through.

45

Plastic explorer balloon

The first passenger-carrying balloon

Weather balloon

Not Quite Planes — Balloons, Blimps and Dirigibles

The first aircraft ever to leave the ground was a balloon. It was filled with heated air, and it rose, empty, more than a mile into the sky, in 1783. Later the same year a balloon carrying a man went up 80 feet. It was 120 years before the first airplane got off the ground.

Balloons are still high fliers. A man-carrying balloon, made of plastic (the first one was linen and paper) and filled with helium, has gone almost 20 miles into the air, and stayed there more than 24 hours. This is so far into space that the sky is almost black. An airplane can't fly this high. Only a rocket has gone higher.

Everyday weather balloons go up from all major weather stations. They carry special equipment that sends messages back to receivers on the ground, reporting on conditions in the upper air, where most weather is made. Balloons are exploring the weather, and the beginning of space. Some carry equipment and some carry men, too; and the things the men and equipment find out will help all the high fliers who are still to come.

Balloons, blimps, and dirigibles have an advantage over planes. They are filled with a gas that makes them lighter than air. They stay up easily. But they cannot go as fast as a plane, and they are clumsier. Blimps and dirigibles are really kinds of balloons. DIRIGIBLES have rigid frames inside the bags, but BLIMPS have no frames at all.

The first airliners were dirigibles. They were in regular service flying the Atlantic, before the first airplane flew across nonstop. But the gas with which they were filled caught fire very easily, and after a series of disasters nobody wanted to fly in dirigibles or even make them.

Blimps are still used by the Navy and Coast Guard, because they fly slowly and quietly. They are filled with helium gas, which will not burn.

There is even talk about lighter-than-air airliners again — slower than airplanes but faster than ships, and quiet as a cloud.

So that air space can be protected, the CAA has rules about operating free balloons, and even very large kites.

Blimp

Dirigible

What Makes an Airplane?

Lots of things make an airplane.

DESIGNERS start a plane. On drawing boards first, many skilled designers work out new designs. Some design shapes, some design engines, some may even design only a wing.

SCIENTISTS make a plane. They work on new combinations of metals, new plastics, and coverings, better fuels, new electronic devices that make planes easier and safer to fly.

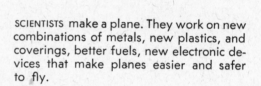

RESEARCH AND TESTING make a plane. Exact scale models are built and tested in wind tunnels like this one, against all the conditions of actual flying — wind, speed, heat, weather. Mistakes are corrected, and the models tried over and over again.

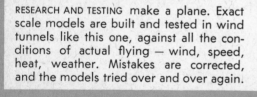

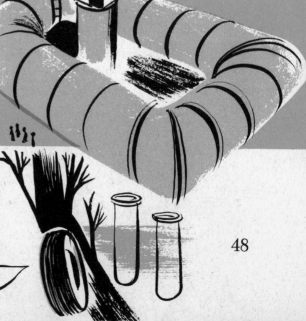

MATERIALS FROM ALL OVER THE WORLD make a plane; metals and rubber, plastics, fuels, glass, wood, and leather, and other things that are still being invented.

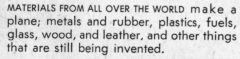

48

TEST PILOTS make a plane. A single model is built, then tested by a pilot whose business it is to know how every part of the plane should react to every test he puts on it. CAA inspectors check the plane for airworthiness from the designing board on. No plane is ever put into production until everything about it has been thoroughly tested.

MACHINES make a plane — huge machines that can stamp out a fuselage in a single operation, others that make electronic parts no bigger than a pinhead.

PEOPLE make a plane: designers, engineers and draftsmen, mechanics and welders, painters and stitchers and secretaries all make planes. The people who fly in them make planes too; we wouldn't need planes if there weren't any passengers.

49

Getting Them Up

Most planes take off from airports. They taxi along the runway into the wind until the thrust from their engines and the lift of the wind across their wings carries them up into the air.

But what if a runway is too short for some planes to get up flying speed? What if there is no runway at all? How do planes get up into the air then?

A helicopter has no problem at all. Because it can take off vertically (straight up), it doesn't need a runway. This take-off method is so handy, designers have worked out other planes that can take off vertically.

They call this a "vertical-rising airplane." Its jet engines point down, so that their thrust lifts the plane straight up. Then the engines can be turned to provide forward thrust. Someday many airplanes may have batteries of downward-pointing jets so that they can take off and land vertically. They would have other engines for flying.

This plane is designed to stand on its tail and climb straight up. Then the pilot turns the plane so it is flying forward.

Some fast jets are actually blasted into the sky by booster rockets that pack ten times the thrust of their own engines.

Some planes can take off almost vertically from launching platforms like this. With a launching platform, the fastest plane could take off anywhere.

Sometimes fast and heavy planes need extra power to help them take off. Extra jet engines can be fastened outside to give more power. Once the plane is in the air, these extra engines drop away. Air men call this JATO, which stands for "jet assisted take-off."

An aircraft carrier is a floating airport. New carriers have a rear deck that is angled, so that planes can land and take off without banging into other planes on the front deck. A series of hooks and wires keeps landing planes from going too far and falling into the water. Since a carrier deck is too short to allow a plane to get up much forward speed, planes are catapulted off. A CATAPULT is like a big slingshot that shoots a plane down a track, into the air.

Battleships and cruisers usually have catapults too, or helicopters or launching platforms.

Planes without Pilots

Some planes fly without pilots, but are guided from the ground or from another plane. Sometimes, using complicated computing machinery inside them, they can guide themselves to their own targets, changing their "minds" whenever it is necessary.

Drones

DRONES are usually ordinary airplanes with their controls so fixed that they can be radio-directed by a pilot in another plane or in a control tower on the ground. Usually the pilot directs a drone by sight. If it is too far away, or the weather is bad, he uses radar. Drones are fitted with cameras and recording instruments that note things down for scientists to study later when the drone is brought in.

Guided Missiles

Some guided missiles are small. Two men can pick them up. Some are huge, and can fly at speeds faster than sound, across oceans and continents. Guided missiles are usually launched by rocket engines. Then ramjet engines take over to drive them.

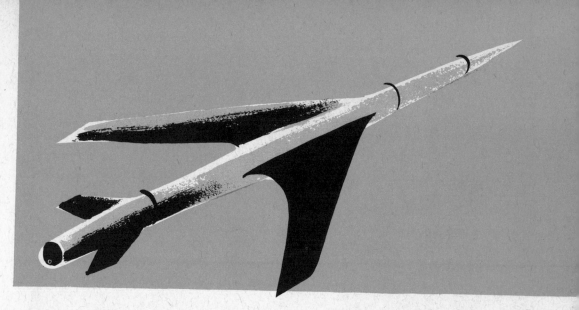

Some guided missiles are controlled from outside, by radar. Others have their own built-in control systems which are set before take-off.

Air experts say that someday all air mail, across continents and oceans, will be carried by these guided rockets. And the descendants of today's missiles may be pilotless airliners, carrying passengers halfway around the world in a few hours.

Rockets

Rockets are our fingers into space. A rocket has gone farther into space than any other manmade thing. Complicated automatic pilots guide them. Radio devices inside them send back to listening stations all kinds of information about the rocket itself and

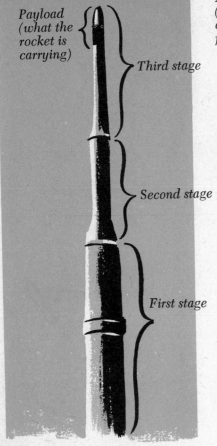

Payload
(what the
rocket is
carrying)

Third stage

Second stage

First stage

A THREE-STAGE ROCKET
(the bottom stages
drop off as their
fuel is used up.)

about the upper atmosphere through which it is flying. Cameras photograph the earth from hundreds of miles above it.

Animals have flown into space aboard a rocket, with instruments recording their reactions, their breathing and heartbeats.

Of all the aircraft we know now, only a rocket can go fast enough to take us out into real space. Rockets have launched instrument-carrying satellites into space, beyond the pull of gravity. The satellites are usually the last stages of the rockets themselves.

Once the satellites are out in space, no instruments guide them. They are like our moon, circling the earth in a regular orbit. They have no power of their own, but are actually falling around the earth.

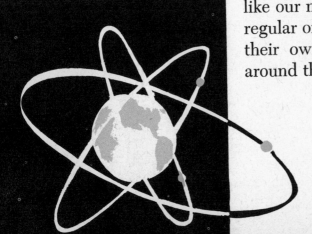

A satellite falls in
an orbit around the
earth. Many orbits are
possible.

54

High-flying pilots are protected by special suits and equipment.

Pilots

Almost anyone can learn to fly, and thousands of people have pilots' licenses. Pilots have to understand their planes, the instruments and engines, and other things too: flying rules, navigation, and something about the weather.

The faster and more complicated a plane is, the more its pilot has to know. He has to be very healthy, because flying at great speeds is hard on a pilot's heart and lungs. He must be able to think and act quickly, because sometimes he has only half a second to make up his mind about something important. Fast flying takes fast thinking.

Pilots are always studying and working and experimenting to get ready for the next step in flying. Orville Wright had to know just what to do for that 12 seconds the first plane was in the air. Now, pilots are studying the problems of flying into space.

55

Helmet of a space suit

How Fast?

The Sound Barrier

The first airplane flew at a speed of 31 miles an hour. Ever since then, planes have been flying faster and faster. Speeds increased until they reached 760 miles an hour. Then a wall stood in the way of the plane — a wall of sound. Scientists called this the SOUND BARRIER.

It is hard to think of a wall of sound, solid enough to keep an airplane from passing it. You can't see sound, or touch it. Sound is made when molecules of air jiggle and push close together so that they travel in little bunches called waves. If you talk, the sound waves travel away from you in all directions.

The sound of a plane's engine travels out away from the plane, *if* the plane is going slower than the sound waves, which move at 760 miles an hour.

But when the plane approaches the speed of sound, all those bunched-up waves of air can't get ahead of it. They pile up in front of it, with the plane trying to push its way through. Before air experts found a way to "break" the sound barrier, a plane would bounce and shake and sometimes even fly apart as it approached the speed of sound. It was as if it really had crashed into something.

Designers had to find new shapes that would help planes cut through the sound barrier. SUPERSONIC (which means "faster than sound") PLANES look different. Their noses are long and sharp. Their wings sweep back. They are designed to slice through the wall of sound instead of banging against it. Once they are through the barrier (and the plane makes a loud *bang* when it goes through), planes can go faster and faster without any trouble because now the sound waves are behind them. When a supersonic plane flies over, it is sometimes out of sight before you ever hear the sound.

The Heat Barrier

(Scientists call this the THERMAL THICKET*)*

Once a pilot has passed the sound barrier, if his engine has enough thrust there is nothing to keep him from going faster and faster — except heat. Heat is made when molecules of air keep bumping into anything very quickly.

The faster a plane cuts through the air, the more the air molecules crowd and bump each other against it.

The speed of sound is called *mach 1.* At *mach* 2, or twice the speed of sound (and many airplanes can fly this fast), the outside metal of the plane can be as hot as 275 degrees Fahrenheit. At *mach* 3, or three times the speed of sound, the temperature of the metal jumps to 675 degrees. This is hot enough to cook the pilot. At *mach* 5, hard steel melts like a marshmallow over a campfire.

All over the world, airplane designers are at work trying to figure out ways to beat the thermal thicket. They are working on new kinds of metals that will resist great heat. They are working on powerful air conditioners to cool every part of the plane. They are working on plane structures which will ward off the fast-moving air molecules.

How Far?

An airplane can fly only as far as its fuel will take it, but it can refuel as it flies. A tanker plane, flying above it, lets down a fuel line and fuel flows into the lower plane's tanks. Large tanker planes can refuel several planes at once.

When atomic engines are built for airplanes, those planes will be able to fly great distances on a tiny bit of fuel, without refueling at all. The plan for an atomic airplane will probably look something like this.

The crew would stay in a heavily shielded compartment.

The atomic reactor (for making atomic energy) would be here.

How High?

So far, we have barely gotten away from the earth's surface. Nobody knows yet how high an airplane can fly. Planes with rocket engines can fly higher than those that need outside oxygen to keep their engines going. New wing designs provide extra lift to keep a plane flying even where the air is very thin. Rockets, which depend on tremendous thrust instead of lift, can fly as high and as far as their thrust will take them.

Nobody knows yet how high people can fly. We are made for living and breathing in the air close to the earth's surface. If we get too far above the earth we need lots of help from science.

We need extra oxygen to breathe. We need the air pressure our bodies are accustomed to. In high-flying airliners the cabins are pressurized and oxygen is continually being pumped in. A pilot who flies higher wears an oxygen mask or a special helmet into which oxygen is being pumped.

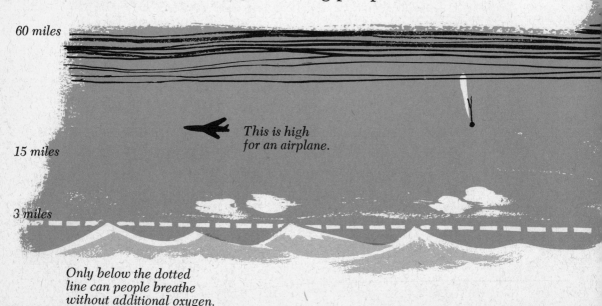

60 miles

15 miles

*This is high
for an airplane.*

3 miles

*Only below the dotted
line can people breathe
without additional oxygen.*

At very high altitudes a pilot must wear a space suit, in which the air pressure is kept at the pressure he is used to on earth. Twenty miles up (and that is hardly approaching *real* space, which begins at over 100 miles), a pilot could not live unless he were in a pressurized suit or cabin.

Nobody knows yet how a man would feel when he got high enough to escape the force of gravity. He would be weightless. He would have to think about breathing and swallowing — things we do automatically on earth. He would have to stand tremendous pressures going up, as the force of gravity tried to pull him back to earth. He would have to stand tremendous buffeting, or shaking, as he tried to re-enter the earth's atmosphere from space.

And still, all over the world pilots are getting ready, and space medicine experts are working on ways to help men live in space. How high? All the way up!

61

New Things

Airplane designers are always working on new ideas so that planes can go higher and faster, be safer and more useful to more people.

The CONVERTIPLANE is a helicopter with fixed wings. It can take off vertically like a helicopter, then fly like an ordinary airplane.

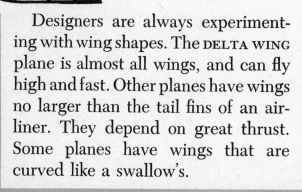

Designers are always experimenting with wing shapes. The DELTA WING plane is almost all wings, and can fly high and fast. Other planes have wings no larger than the tail fins of an airliner. They depend on great thrust. Some planes have wings that are curved like a swallow's.

This ONE-MAN HELICOPTER is hardly more than a flying chair. Someday you may even have a plane you can carry on your back.

There is an airplane designed to take men up through the atmosphere and out into space. It has standard controls that will be used for flying through the earth's atmosphere. Above the atmosphere, where there is no air, small reaction engines in its wings and fuselage will allow the pilot to maneuver his ship.

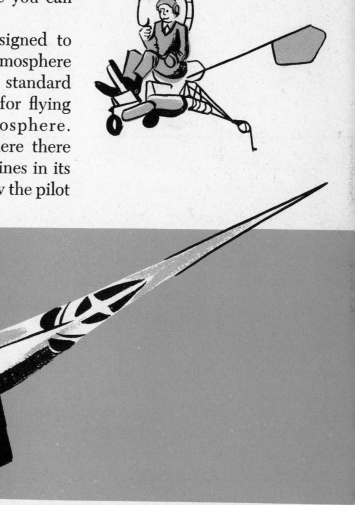

Someday, not too far away, air travel and space travel will shake hands.

Index